CAPE VERDE
TRAVEL GUI
BEGINNERS

The Updated Concise Guide for Planning a Trip to Cape Verde Including Top Destinations,Culture,Outdoor Activities,Dining,Cuisine and Getting Around

Thanh Minick

TABLE OF CONTENT

CHAPTER 1

INTRODUCTION

Cape Verde, a stunning archipelago located off the western coast of Africa, entices travellers with its distinctive combination of appealing geographical features, culturally significant history, and lively indigenous populations. This introduction provides an entry point to the captivating realm of Cape Verde, revealing its geographical importance, intricate historical fabric, and the factors contributing to its growing popularity as a sought-after tourism destination.

Located in the Atlantic Ocean, Cape Verde has 10 main islands and several smaller islets, each with unique characteristics and attractions. The archipelago's geographically advantageous position has long rendered it a crucial hub for maritime traffic between Europe, Africa, and the Americas. The landscape of the islands exhibits a remarkable diversity, including the magnificent volcanic highlands of Santo Antão and the sun-drenched beaches of Sal and Boa Vista. This diverse range of options allows travellers to partake in a multitude of activities, including anything from exhilarating treks to tranquil beach getaways, all within a compact geographical expanse.

Upon closer examination of Cape Verde's historical narrative, one discovers a rich tapestry interwoven with tales of tenacity and the amalgamation of many cultural elements. The archipelago was first seen by the Portuguese around the 15th century, subsequently becoming into a pivotal hub for commerce and cultural exchange across Europe, Africa, and the Americas. The cultural amalgamation is clearly seen in the music, dance, food, and language of the archipelago, thereby leaving a lasting impact on its heritage. The musical traditions of Cape Verde, namely the expressive tunes of morna and the lively cadences of coladeira, serve as a manifestation of the intricate historical background of the nation and the profound emotional experiences of its inhabitants. The lyrical content often encompasses dramatic narratives centred around themes of love, yearning, and the complex and ambivalent aspects of human existence.

In recent times, Cape Verde has transitioned from its historical context and has gained popularity as a very desirable tourism destination, with valid reasons. The archipelago has a remarkable array of natural aesthetics, accommodating a broad spectrum of individual inclinations. The sandy coasts of Sal and Boa Vista provide an ideal setting for those who have a strong affinity for beaches. These locations provide opportunities for relaxing, engaging in water sports, and experiencing lively nightlife. On the other hand, those with a penchant for adventure have the opportunity to engage in the exploration of the challenging topography of Santo Antão by means of traversing trekking routes that meander through valleys, summits, and picturesque settlements. Each island has distinct characteristics that contribute to its own allure, exemplified by the vibrant cultural milieu of Mindelo on São Vicente and the quaint hamlet harmoniously tucked within the volcanic topography of Fogo.

The weather in Cape Verde is an additional factor that attracts tourists throughout the year. Featuring a favourable tropical environment and a regularly elevated temperature, this destination serves as an attractive sanctuary for those seeking respite from colder geographical regions. The dry season, which occurs from November to June, is highly favoured by tourists due to its suitability for exploring the outdoor attractions of the islands without the inconvenience of excessive rainfall.

Furthermore, the inhabitants of Cape Verde exhibit a kind disposition towards tourists, graciously imparting their rich cultural legacy and traditions with a welcoming spirit. The indigenous inhabitants of the region, often referred to as Cabo Verdeans, are renowned for their warm reception of visitors and their dynamic cultural practises. Interacting with the local inhabitants offers tourists a more profound comprehension of the archipelago's cultural practises and their gradual transformation across many generations. The traditional markets of Cape Verde provide a platform for cultural interaction and facilitate the acquisition of vivid fabrics, detailed crafts, and fresh vegetables, enabling visitors to bring a tangible representation of Cape Verde's essence to their own homes.

When embarking on a visit to Cape Verde, it is important to recognise the archipelago's importance beyond just a visually appealing tourist destination. Cape Verde serves as a tangible example of the strength of perseverance, the blending of many cultures, and the inherent beauty of its natural surroundings. The archipelago's capacity to provide a range of experiences, including serene beach getaways and invigorating treks over volcanic landscapes, is indicative of its complex nature. Cape Verde caters to a diverse range of travellers, providing opportunities for leisure, adventure, cultural immersion, or a combination thereof. Prepare yourself for an immersive journey where the realms of history, nature, and culture seamlessly converge, resulting in an indelible travel encounter.

CHAPTER 2

Exploring the Islands of Cape Verde

Cape Verde, including 10 primary islands and several islets dispersed throughout the expansive Atlantic Ocean, is an enticing destination for those in search of a distinctive amalgamation of scenic splendour, cultural opulence, and engaging encounters. Each of the islands has a unique and individualistic character, providing a diverse selection of activities, sceneries, and traditions that appeal to a broad spectrum of interests. Undertaking an expedition to investigate these islands is like to revealing a vibrant tapestry interwoven with the strands of historical, natural, and cultural elements.

1. Santiago: A City Immersed in Historical Significance

Santiago, the most extensive and densely populated of the Cape Verdean islands, is a dynamic amalgamation of historical importance and contemporary existence. Praia, the capital of the island, functions as a significant centre for both cultural and political activities, characterised by a fusion of architectural styles from the colonial period and modern times. Cidade Velha, a village located on the island of Santiago, has the distinction of being recognised as a UNESCO World Heritage site. Historically, this town had a prominent role as a hub for transatlantic slave traffic. The cobblestone alleys, fortifications, and cathedrals of the area provide as tangible evidence of a multifaceted historical narrative that intricately weaves together African, European, and Creole cultural influences.

2. Sal and Boa Vista: An Exploration of Sun, Sand, and Seascapes

Sal and Boa Vista are ideal destinations for those in search of sun-drenched beaches and engaging in water sports activities. Sal, renowned for its lively resort scene, has pristine seas that are ideal for engaging in activities like as swimming, snorkelling, and diving. The Pedra de Lume site, which was once used as a salt mine but has now transformed into a natural salt pond, presents an exceptional prospect for individuals to engage in a buoyant swimming experience among its lunar-esque surroundings.

In contrast, Boa Vista has an alluring appeal via its expansive and unspoiled sand dunes, which serve to enhance its serene aesthetic. The island serves as a habitat for loggerhead turtles, who use it as a nesting site. Visitors have the opportunity to engage in guided excursions, during which they may see the awe-inspiring phenomenon of these turtles depositing their eggs. Sal Rei, a town that offers a glimpse into Cape Verdean culture, showcases vibrant marketplaces, classic architectural structures, and a leisurely atmosphere that embodies the laid-back ambiance of the archipelago.

3. São Vicente: A Hub of Cultural Significance

São Vicente, characterised by its vibrant urban centre, Mindelo, serves as a cultural hub where the realms of music, art, and celebration converge. Mindelo is well noted for its vibrant music culture, characterised by the regular occurrence of live performances including morna, coladeira, and several other traditional genres, permeating the atmosphere throughout the city. The presence of colonial-era architecture and bustling marketplaces in the city contributes to an ambiance that is imbued with a sense of authenticity.

4. Santo Antão: A Remarkable Display of Nature's Splendour

Santo Antão is an idyllic destination for those with a passion for nature and a thirst for adventure. The region's topography is characterised by its harsh and elevated landscape, which offers awe-inspiring hiking routes that meander over valleys, ravines, and charming settlements. The island is often known as the Hiker's Paradise due to the presence of routes like the Paul Valley route, which provide extensive vistas of verdant landscapes and terraced farms. In this location, individuals have the opportunity to fully engage with an environment where conventional agricultural methods and breathtaking landscapes intersect.

5. Fogo Island: A Geological Wonder

Fogo, the volcanic island that has significant symbolic value throughout the archipelago, serves as a tangible representation of the dynamic and evolving geographical features of Cape Verde. The prominent feature of the island's landscape is the imposing stratovolcano known as Pico do Fogo. The landscape of this region exhibits extraordinary characteristics that highlight the dual forces of nature, including both its capacity for devastation and its ability to foster growth. The juxtaposition of lava fields beside verdant valleys serves as a vivid representation of this phenomenon. São Filipe, a town known for its colonial elegance, offers visitors a unique opportunity to explore the historical and cultural legacy of the island.

6. Maio, São Nicolau, Brava, and the Islets: Lesser-Known Treasures

The islands of Maio, São Nicolau, Brava, and their adjacent islets are characterised by their relatively low levels of visitation, hence providing a more unconventional and less frequented travel experience. Maio is renowned for its unspoiled beaches, natural scenery, and an atmosphere of serenity that epitomises the more calm aspect of Cape Verde. São Nicolau has a range of striking natural features and varied topography, including the rich Ribeira

Brava valley and the visually captivating settlement of Tarrafal. Brava, the least populous of the inhabited islands, is renowned for its abundant botanical and zoological diversity, characterised by flourishing gardens, picturesque settlements, and a tranquil atmosphere.

7. Exploring the Multifaceted Nature of Cultural Diversity

In addition to their scenic beauty, the islands of Cape Verde are enriched with a diverse cultural tapestry that reflects the archipelago's historical and heritage significance. Traditional markets provide as a valuable platform for craftsmen and traders to showcase their complex crafts, fabrics, and locally sourced goods, so offering observers a glimpse into the fabric of daily life. Cape Verdean cuisine exhibits a harmonious amalgamation of African, European, and Portuguese elements, whereby notable culinary expressions such as cachupa, a robust stew, and the utilisation of fresh seafood encapsulate the islands' gastronomic character.

8. Embracing the Concept of Responsible Tourism

When engaging in the exploration of the islands' many attractions, it is of utmost importance to adopt and adhere to responsible tourism principles. The conservation and preservation of Cape Verde's sensitive ecosystems and distinct cultures are deserving of attention and prioritisation. Sustainable exploration is facilitated via active involvement with local people, demonstrating respect for their cultural practises, and adopting measures to mitigate environmental harm.

Undertaking an expedition to investigate the archipelago of Cape Verde may be likened to entering a multifaceted realm of diverse encounters. Each island in the archipelago contributes its own distinct colour to the colourful palette of Cape Verde, ranging from the historical importance of Santiago to the sun-drenched beaches of Sal and Boa Vista, and from the cultural energy of São Vicente to the natural grandeur of Santo Antão and Fogo. Cape Verde's islands provide a diverse and comprehensive experience for travellers, including opportunities for leisure, adventure, cultural immersion, or a combination thereof. This voyage has a lasting impact on the emotional and spiritual aspects of individuals, leaving an enduring impression on their hearts and souls.

CHAPTER 3

Accommodation Options in Cape Verde

Cape Verde, an archipelago renowned for its diverse cultural heritage, breathtaking natural scenery, and lively ambiance, has a wide range of lodging choices tailored to different traveller tastes and financial capacities. The diverse range of accommodations available, including luxurious resorts and lovely guesthouses, offers distinct avenues for individuals to immerse themselves in the islands' hospitality and allure, all while enjoying the luxuries and conveniences provided.

1. Luxury Resorts: Unmatched Sophistication and Extensive Facilities

Cape Verde's luxury resorts provide a lavish retreat for discerning travellers, allowing them to immerse themselves in stunning natural settings while indulging in unparalleled opulence. These resorts, often situated along unspoiled coastlines or with scenic views, provide a variety of luxurious features such as exclusive swimming pools, wellness facilities, high-quality eating establishments, and tailored hospitality services.

2. Boutique Hotels: The Allure of Intimacy and Genuine Experiences Boutique hotels have gained popularity in recent years due to their unique characteristics that provide a distinct charm and provide guests with authentic experiences. These establishments, often characterised by their small size and personalised service, have become a preferred choice for travellers seeking a more intimate and immersive stay. By

Boutique hotels are a preferred option for those who prioritise individualised service and a more intimate atmosphere. These institutions often include distinctive motifs that are indicative of the indigenous culture and historical background of Cape Verde. Visitors may anticipate a pleasant lodging experience, individualised attention, and the chance to fully engage with the island's allure via authentically influenced interior design, artwork, and culinary options.

3. Guesthouses and Bed & Breakfasts: Embodying Local Culture and Offering Genuine Hospitality

Guesthouses and bed & breakfast establishments provide travellers an opportunity to experience the original Cape Verdean lifestyle and genuine local friendliness. Typically, these smaller institutions are operated by families, so guaranteeing a hospitable reception and an opportunity for intimate engagement with the local community. Visitors have the opportunity to engage in a collective ambiance, fostering the exchange of narratives and recommendations among other sojourners. Additionally, they may indulge in delectable breakfasts prepared in-house, which serve as a representation of the distinctive tastes found around the archipelago.

4. Self-catering accommodations, such as apartments and villas, provide a flexible and homely alternative to traditional lodging options.

Self-catering apartments and villas are a favourable option for those seeking more autonomy and adaptability throughout their travels. These lodgings are equipped with kitchen facilities, enabling visitors to independently make their meals and have the opportunity to savour the culinary pleasures of Cape Verde at their own convenience. Families or social units might discover expansive accommodations that provide the convenience and familiarity akin to a domicile in a different location.

5. Sustainable Lodges: Achieving Environmental Harmony

The dedication of Cape Verde to the principles of sustainable tourism is evident in the presence of environmentally conscious resorts and lodgings within its territory. These businesses endeavour to minimise their ecological footprint while offering excellent accommodations. Visitors have the opportunity to appreciate tranquil environments, participate in ecologically sustainable pursuits, and actively support the conservation of the islands' distinct ecosystems.

6. Local Inns and Pousadas: A Cultural Immersion Experience in Cape Verde

The local inns and pousadas in Cape Verde provide a unique combination of simplicity and authenticity, enabling travellers to intimately engage with the local culture of the region. These cost-effective alternatives often provide fundamental conveniences while providing tourists with an authentic experience of the local culture. Opting to stay in a pousada provides travellers with an opportunity to establish a connection with the Cape Verdean essence and actively participate in community engagement.

7. The Role of Campsites and Glamping in Cultivating a Spirit of Exploration

Cape Verde has campsites and glamping options that cater to those seeking adventurous experiences, enabling them to establish a distinctive connection with the natural environment. Engaging in the activity of camping under the celestial expanse of starlit heavens, whether it be on secluded coastal shores or amongst awe-inspiring natural environments, has the potential to bestow upon individuals an indelible encounter with unadulterated aesthetics and serenity.

8. Selecting the Appropriate Accommodation

The process of choosing suitable lodging in Cape Verde is contingent upon personal preferences, trip objectives, and financial constraints. Luxury resorts are very desirable for those in search of an opulent retreat characterised by exceptional facilities and services. Boutique hotels and guesthouses are establishments that specifically cater to the preferences of travellers that value a more intimate and personalised experience, want to immerse themselves in the local culture, and actively participate with the local community. Self-catering accommodations, such as flats and villas, provide individuals with the advantage of convenience and autonomy, allowing them to have control over their own meals and daily routines. On the other hand, eco-friendly lodges respond to the growing demand for sustainable practises, aligning with individuals' views of environmental responsibility.

9. Experience the Cultural Immersion in Cape Verde

Irrespective of the selected style of lodging, tourists visiting Cape Verde have the opportunity to completely engage with the cultural and societal aspects of the archipelago. Engaging in interactions with local residents, partaking in traditional gastronomy, and exploring local markets all enhance one's comprehension of the culture and legacy that characterise these islands.

10. The Importance of Responsible Travel and Cultural Respect

When partaking in the hospitality of Cape Verde, it is essential to exhibit proper behaviour as a traveller. The preservation of the islands' distinctive beauty and culture for future generations is facilitated by the adherence to local traditions, the conservation of resources, and the minimization of waste.

In conclusion, Cape Verde offers a wide array of lodging choices that respond to the individual interests of every traveller, ensuring a harmonious combination of comfort, cultural genuineness, and the unique attractiveness of the islands. Whether engaging in opulence or embracing modesty, each decision provides an entry point to the archipelago's rich cultural heritage, awe-inspiring natural scenery, and kind reception.

CHAPTER 4

Cuisine and Dining

Cape Verde, an archipelago situated in the Atlantic Ocean, enthrals tourists not alone due to its breathtaking scenery and lively cultural scene, but also because to its abundant and varied gastronomy. Cape Verdean cuisine is characterised by a rich amalgamation of African, Portuguese, and Creole culinary traditions, serving as a vibrant manifestation of the archipelago's historical, geographical, and cultural synthesis. Embarking on a gastronomic exploration of Cape Verde entails immersing oneself in a realm where materials serve as narratives, and every culinary creation encapsulates the distinctive spirit of the archipelago's personality.

1. A Multifaceted Culinary Tapestry: Examining Influences on Gastronomy

The culinary traditions of Cape Verde reflect its historical associations and multifaceted influences. The geographical location of the islands facilitated its role as a pivotal point for commerce, resulting in the introduction of diverse foodstuffs from various parts of the globe. Consequently, these ingredients have significantly influenced the flavour profiles that are emblematic of Cape Verdean cuisine. The integration of African staples, including maize, beans and cassava, with Portuguese components like as fish, shellfish, olive oil and a variety of spices, results in a harmonic culinary fusion.

2. Fresh Seafood: The Culinary Centrepiece

Due to Cape Verde's geographical proximity to the shore, it is not unexpected that seafood plays a prominent role in its culinary traditions. Freshly caught fish such as tuna, wahoo, and grouper are sourced from the adjacent seas and are often consumed by both local inhabitants and tourists. The dish known as Cachupa de Peixe exemplifies the island's affinity for seafood and its adeptness in elevating basic components into delectable culinary creations. This substantial fish stew, prepared by simmering an assortment of vegetables and spices, serves as a testament to the island's culinary prowess.

3. Cachupa: An Iconic Culinary Dish

Cachupa, a traditional dish, has significant cultural and historical value in its role as a culinary emblem.

Cachupa, a stew renowned as Cape Verde's quintessential culinary representation, embodies the historical and gastronomic essence of the archipelago. This culinary creation exemplifies the ingenuity of Cape Verdeans, since it emerged from the need to use accessible products. The stew often comprises of ingredients such as maize, beans, vegetables and a variety of meats, which are frequently cooked at a low temperature for an extended period of time, resulting in a culinary creation that elicits feelings of comfort and profound contentment. Cachupa has regional variations throughout all the islands, whereby each locality contributes its own culinary nuances to this staple dish.

4. The Abundance of Fruits and Vegetables on Islands

Despite the dry environment of the islands, Cape Verde exhibits a remarkable variety of fresh fruits and vegetables. Tropical fruits such as papaya, banana, and guava exhibit robust growth in the rich valleys of certain islands. Catchupa Rica, a modified rendition of the conventional cachupa, accentuates the utilisation of locally cultivated products by integrating an increased assortment of vegetables and fruits, so yielding a more opulent and multifaceted taste composition.

5. Traditional Beverages: Satiating Thirst and Commemorating Cultural Heritage

In addition to its culinary offerings, Cape Verde has a selection of traditional drinks that serve as reflections of the archipelago's rich culture and past. The beverage known as Grogue is a popular local spirit derived from the fermentation of sugarcane. It is often consumed at communal meetings and festive occasions. Another customary beverage is Ponche, which is a fusion of grogue, condensed milk, sugar, and spices that evokes the historical legacy of the islands' colonial era.

6. The Culinary Pleasures of Street Food: Exploring the Everyday Gastronomy

For anyone seeking an authentic immersion into local culinary traditions and the everyday routines of Cape Verde, it is essential to embark on an exploration of the vibrant street food culture in the region. Pastéis, which are deep-fried pastries filled with a variety of ingredients such as fish, pork, or cheese, have gained popularity as a favoured snack among both local inhabitants and tourists. These palatable delicacies provide a convenient and flavorful glimpse into the culinary heritage of Cape Verde while meandering through the lively thoroughfares.

7. Dining Experiences: Exploring Local Eateries and Upscale Restaurants

Cape Verde has a diverse selection of eating options that cater to a wide variety of interests and financial capacities. Traditional Tabernas are establishments that are often found in small communities and provide cooked meals. These establishments provide an opportunity for travellers to experience and enjoy real cuisine in a humble and unpretentious setting. High-end dining establishments, often situated in opulent resorts or metropolitan regions, exhibit the culinary expertise of the islands via innovative renditions of customary dishes, complemented with a hint of global influence.

8. The Role of Food in Facilitating Cultural Exchange

Cape Verdean food serves as more than just nutrition, functioning as a cultural conduit that fosters intergenerational connections, upholds traditional practises, and strengthens communal bonds. Partaking in a culinary experience in Cape Verde offers an opportunity to delve into the essence of the archipelago's culture, characterised by the sharing of narratives, the establishment of interpersonal connections, and the formation of lasting impressions.

9. Responsible Exploration of Culinary Traditions

When indulging in the culinary delights of Cape Verde, it is imperative to exercise responsible consumption. The promotion of local markets, the protection of the environment, and active community engagement, along with waste reduction efforts, together contribute to the sustainable development and preservation of the islands.

In summary, the culinary panorama of Cape Verde is a manifestation of its historical, geographical, and cultural heterogeneity. The culinary offerings of the islands include a wide array of flavours and cultural significance, ranging from the bountiful selection of fresh seafood to the nourishing qualities of cachupa, a traditional meal. Additionally, the local drinks serve as a pleasant accompaniment to these gastronomic delights. Each dish serves as a narrative, encapsulating the spirit and heritage of the islands. Appreciating the culinary offerings of Cape Verde extends beyond just sustenance, as it entails engaging with a diverse range of flavours that intricately shape the archipelago's distinct character. Each dining experience becomes an enriching journey that celebrates the cultural and traditional heritage of this island nation.

CHAPTER 5

Cultural Experiences

Cape Verde, an archipelago situated in the Atlantic Ocean, is well known for its picturesque scenery and attractive beaches, as well as its extensive and varied cultural legacy. Upon arrival, travellers are presented with an opportunity to start on a profound exploration of Cape Verdean culture, characterised by a rich amalgamation of music, dance, festivals, and engaging encounters with the hospitable local population. Cape Verde offers a diverse range of cultural experiences that engage the senses and foster enduring relationships, including the melodic rhythms of traditional music and the vibrant street festivals that imbue the local atmosphere.

1. Music: The Melodious Soundscapes of Cape Verde

Music plays an indisputably central role in Cape Verdean culture, permeating every facet of the islands with its melodious essence. The archipelago has contributed to the global cultural landscape with the emergence of the expressive genre of morna, a soulful type of music sometimes compared to the blues. Morna serves as a comprehensive representation of the fundamental aspects of Cape Verdean culture, effectively recounting narratives that revolve around themes of affection, yearning, and the many emotional experiences inherent in human existence. Coladeira, a vibrant kind of dance music, serves as a captivating rhythmic gem that entices both residents and tourists to sway to its infectious melodies. Participating in various local music events, ranging from spontaneous jam sessions to organised concerts, offers a distinct avenue for individuals to establish a profound connection with the essence of Cape Verdean culture.

2. Dance: Dynamic Movements and Expressive Gestures Dance is an art form that encompasses a wide range of vibrant movements and expressive gestures. It serves as a means of communication and self-expression, allowing individuals to convey emotions, stories, and ideas via physicality. The

Dance has a significant role within the cultural fabric of Cape Verde, fostering communal gatherings that serve as occasions for celebration, social bonding, and the articulation of emotional states.

Funaná, a dance form characterised by its quick tempo and powerful movements, encapsulates the dynamic essence of the islands. The batuque dance, renowned for its rhythmic movements and mesmerising chanting, provides insight into the longstanding traditions of the archipelago. Engaging in a dance session with local residents offers an opportunity to personally encounter the dynamic and cohesive essence that dance imbues into the cultural fabric of Cape Verde.

3. Festivals and Celebrations: An Exuberant Fabric of Cultural Expression

The calendar of Cape Verde is characterised by a diverse array of festivals and festivities that commemorate the islands' cultural history, religious practises, and social cohesion. Carnival, an enthusiastic cultural event characterised by brilliant and colourful displays, encompasses the streets via the use of extravagant costumes, parades, and lively music. The Sao João Festival, an annual event taking place in the month of June, serves as a platform for the convergence of European and African cultural practises. This celebration is characterised by vibrant street festivities, the participation of local residents in traditional sports, and the lighting of bonfires. These festivals not only give an opportunity to get insight into the cultural richness of Cape Verde but also allow individuals to partake in the collective experience of unity and jubilation.

4. The Significance of Artisan Craftsmanship: A Journey from Hands to Hearts

The artists of Cape Verde skillfully incorporate narratives into their crafts, resulting in elaborate creations that serve as a testament to the islands' rich historical and cultural heritage. The native handicraft of Cape Verde is characterised by a diverse range of artistic expressions, including vivid fabrics and intricately hand-carved sculptures. These artistic manifestations serve as a reflection of the cultural essence and identity of the region. By actively participating in workshops with craftsmen or immersing oneself in local markets, individuals may get valuable insights into the intricate creative processes involved in crafting these valuable artefacts. Moreover, this experiential engagement enables individuals to acquire physical mementos that embody the rich cultural heritage of the islands.

5. The Importance of Community Engagement: Facilitating the Exchange of Narratives and Establishing Interconnections

Cape Verdeans are renowned for their amiable hospitality and authentic interpersonal exchanges, so transforming each conversation into an opportunity for profound connection. The act of engaging in talks with individuals from the local community, exchanging personal narratives at a shared meal, or actively participating in communal gatherings contributes to the formation of enduring memories and facilitates the development of cross-cultural comprehension. Engaging in activities such as participating in a local football match, assisting in traditional cuisine, or engaging in emotional conversations fosters a feeling of inclusion and gratitude towards Cape Verde's hospitable nature among travellers.

6. Language and Expression: The Influence of Linguistic Communication

Language functions as a conduit that facilitates intercultural communication, enabling individuals who are traversing different cultural contexts to establish more profound connections with local inhabitants and get a deeper understanding of their customs and lifestyles. The official language of Cape Verde is Portuguese, but, the presence of many native languages, such as Cape Verdean Creole, serves as a reflection of the archipelago's eclectic heritage. Acquiring a basic understanding of certain expressions in Creole may significantly contribute to establishing strong interpersonal ties and demonstrating a genuine appreciation for the indigenous culture.

7. Ethical Cultural Exploration: The Importance of Tradition Preservation

When participating in cultural activities, it is essential to approach them with a mindset of respect and responsibility. The preservation and continuance of Cape Verde's unique culture may be facilitated via the observance of local traditions, the practise of obtaining permission prior to capturing photographs, and the active support of local artists and craftsmen.

The cultural experiences of Cape Verde provide an opportunity for travellers to get insight into the essence of the archipelago, allowing them to immerse themselves in its diverse and vibrant fabric. The Cape

Verdean cultural landscape is characterised by a diverse range of experiences that contribute to its dynamic and multifaceted nature. These include the evocative melodies of morna and the energetic rhythms of coladeira, as well as dance-filled festivities and touching contacts with the local population. Each of these encounters serves to enrich the cultural mosaic that distinguishes Cape Verde. As individuals embark on their journeys, immersing themselves in the melodies, movements, celebrations, and narratives of the islands, they establish meaningful bonds that beyond geographical boundaries. Consequently, they depart with treasured recollections and an enhanced admiration for the splendour inherent in cultural multiplicity.

CHAPTER 6

Outdoor Activities

Cape Verde, an archipelago located in the Atlantic Ocean, offers a variety of landscapes and outdoor activities for anyone interested in adventure and nature. The archipelago provides an opportunity for individuals to engage with the natural environment and partake in memorable outdoor activities, owing to its mountainous terrain, vibrant turquoise seas, and scenic beaches.

1. Trekking and Hiking: Exploring Trails of Knowledge

For those who get pleasure from the excitement of adventure, Cape Verde's walking and hiking paths provide an optimal opportunity to uncover the islands' hidden gems. Santo Antão is often recognised as an ideal destination for hiking enthusiasts due to its extensive system of pathways that traverse vibrant valleys, abundant canyons, and charming settlements. The Paul Valley trail provides awe-inspiring vistas of agricultural terraces and striking landscapes, while the Cova Crater Trail reveals a fantastical realm nestled inside the core of the mountains. These routes provide not only physical obstacles but also the benefit of panoramic views that showcase the natural beauty of the archipelago.

2. Aquatic Recreational Activities: Surfing, Scuba Diving, and Beyond

Cape Verde's pristine seas and reliable wave conditions make it an ideal destination for aficionados of water sports. The archipelago is increasingly becoming acknowledged as a prominent surfing destination, drawing surfers from many parts of the world to experience and navigate its formidable waves. The island of Sal is renowned for its surfing locations, providing prospects for individuals at all skill levels, ranging from novices to experienced surfers. In addition to the recreational activities of surfing, snorkelling, and scuba diving, there exists a diverse and lively underwater ecosystem characterised by an abundance of marine organisms, coral reefs, and sunken vessels, all of which beckon investigation under the ocean's surface.

3. Windsurfing and Kitesurfing: Harnessing the Power of Trade Winds Windsurfing and kitesurfing are two popular water sports that rely on the utilisation of trade winds. These activities include riding on a board while being propelled by the force of the

wind. Both sports need skill, balance, and technique to navigate the water effectively

Cape Verde's favourable trade winds and optimal environmental conditions make it an ideal destination for aficionados of windsurfing and kitesurfing. The islands of Sal and Boa Vista have expansive sandy coastlines and reliable wind conditions, so creating an ideal environment for engaging in exhilarating activities. Windsurfers and kitesurfers partake in a captivating experience that seamlessly merges the excitement of the sport with the awe-inspiring aesthetics of the environment, whether they are gracefully gliding over the water's surface or soaring above the waves.

4. The Observation of Whales and Interactions with Marine Life

The maritime ecosystem around Cape Verde has a rich diversity of species, giving it an ideal setting for engaging in activities such as whale watching and encountering other forms of marine life. During the period spanning from January to April, humpback whales engage in a migratory behaviour within this aquatic region, therefore presenting an enthralling exhibition of breaching and playful activities. The waterways of this region are inhabited by dolphins, loggerhead turtles, and a diverse array of fish species. Consequently, there are chances for environmentally conscious boat trips that provide both exciting wildlife encounters and valuable knowledge about the archipelago's marine conservation initiatives.

5. Desert Expeditions: Sand Dunes and Off-Road Exploration

The distinctive topography of Cape Verde extends beyond its coastal areas to include its arid regions. The islands of Sal and Boa Vista are distinguished by expansive sand dunes that elicit a sense of ethereal magnificence. Adventurers have the opportunity to participate in off-road expeditions that navigate through visually captivating terrains, using 4x4 vehicles or participating in guided quad bike trips to traverse the dunes. These expeditions provide a striking juxtaposition to the verdant valleys and scenic coastlines, presenting a comprehensive investigation of the varied topography found within the archipelago.

6. Turtle Nesting and Conservation Initiatives

The beaches of Cape Verde serve as both recreational areas and significant breeding grounds for loggerhead turtles. Observing the awe-inspiring phenomenon of these magnificent animals engaging in the process of egg-laying, as well as witnessing the subsequent journey of the hatchlings towards the ocean, elicits a profound sense of humility among individuals, establishing a profound connection between travellers and the intricate equilibrium of the natural world. Several islands, including Boa Vista, provide guided tours facilitated by local conservation organisations, enabling tourists to participate in responsible turtle observation while also contributing to crucial conservation initiatives.

Title: Stargazing: An Exploration of the Celestial Symphony Stargazing has long been a popular activity among those seeking to connect with the celestial realm. This captivating pastime offers a unique opportunity to

The distant and unspoiled landscapes of Cape Verde provide optimal circumstances for seeing celestial phenomena and establishing a connection with the celestial marvels that exist in the sky. In the absence of significant light pollution and under conditions of clear nocturnal atmospheres, the archipelago assumes the role of a blank canvas, upon which celestial bodies like as stars, planets, and constellations manifest themselves in a vivid and animated manner. Participating in stargazing excursions, whether under the guidance of experts or independently, offers individuals the opportunity to reflect upon the immense expanse of the cosmos and examine their own position within it.

When engaging in outdoor activities in Cape Verde, it is essential to exercise responsible behaviour by demonstrating respect for the environment and local populations. By following to established rules for eco-friendly practises, providing support to local conservation initiatives, and upholding responsible tourism principles, individuals may actively contribute to the long-term preservation of the islands' natural marvels, ensuring their protection for future generations.

The outdoor activities of Cape Verde provide a sanctuary of adventure and aesthetic appeal, enticing individuals to transcend conventional experiences and embrace exceptional opportunities. Engaging in various activities like as walking through awe-inspiring mountains, surfing on ocean waves, exploring underwater ecosystems, or stargazing, allows individuals to discover distinct aspects of the archipelago's diverse characteristics. As individuals participate in outdoor activities and explore the landscapes of Cape Verde, they actively contribute to a narrative that appreciates the aesthetic qualities of the natural environment, the exhilaration of discovery, and the deep connection between human beings and the natural world.

THE END

Printed in Great Britain
by Amazon

42456944R00036